SUPER HUMANS

First published in 2012 by
Miles Kelly Publishing Ltd
Harding's Barn, Bardfield End Green,
Thaxted, Essex, CM6 3PX, UK

Copyright © Miles Kelly Publishing Ltd 2011
This edition printed 2013

10 9 8 7 6 5 4 3 2

Publishing Director Belinda Gallagher
Creative Director Jo Cowan
Managing Editors Amanda Askew, Rosie McGuire
Managing Designer Simon Lee
Proofreaders Carly Blake, Claire Philip
Production Manager Elizabeth Collins
Image Manager Liberty Newton
Reprographics Stephan Davis
Assets Lorraine King

All rights reserved. No part of this publication may be reproduced, stored in a retrieval system, or transmitted by any means, electronic, mechanical, photocopying, recording or otherwise, without the prior permission of the copyright holder.

ISBN 978-1-84810-695-6

Printed in China

British Library Cataloguing-in-Publication Data
A catalogue record for this book is available from the British Library

Made with paper from a sustainable forest

www.mileskelly.net
info@mileskelly.net

www.factsforprojects.com

ACKNOWLEDGMENTS

The publishers would like to thank the following sources for the use of their photographs:

KEY Dreamstime=D, Fotolia=F, Getty Images=GI, naturepl.com/Nature Picture Library=NPL, Photolibrary=P, Rex Features=RF, Science Photo Library=SPL, Shutterstock=S
t=top, a=above, b=bottom/below, c=center, l=left, r=right, f=far, m=main, bg=background

COVER moodboard/Corbis **BACK COVER** Zdorov Kirill Vladimirovich/S
1 Kazela/S 2 Pedro Nogueira/S 3(bg) AHMAD FAIZAL YAHYA/S (strip, left to right) Pascal RATEAU/S, Asianet-Pakistan/S, Luciano Mortula/S, Marcel Jancovic/S, markrhiggins/S 4–5 Stringer/india/Reuters/Corbis
6–7(m) Sebastian Derungs/AFP/GI 6(t) Hal_P/S, (bl) Parrot Pascal/Corbis Sygma/Corbis, (candles br) DVARG/S, (cake br) Susan McKenzie/S 7(l) GI, (b) AFP/GI, (c) John T Takai/S, (r) Bettmann/Corbis 8–9(m) Daniel H Bailey/P 8(bl) Darren Staples/Reuters/Corbis 9(tl) Digital Vision/GI, (tr) AFP/GI, (b) Wang Song/Xinhua Press/Corbis 10(t) Monkey Business Images/S, (c) Hung Chung Chih/S, (cb) jovannig/S, (bl) Laitr Keiows/S, (br) Alangh/D 11(t) jan kranendonk/S, (c) Kaido Karner/S, (b) Nikola Spasenoski/S 10–1(globe l, t–b) Steve Estvanik/S, Alvin Ganesh/S, Dmitry Nikolaev/F, PavelSvoboda/S, (globe c, t–b) Nikola Spasenoski/S, BartlomiejMagierowski/S, Elenathewise/F, (globe r, t–b) Pichugin Dmitry/S, Steve Estvanik/S 12(m and inset) Bryan and Cherry Alexander/NPL, (b) hoboton/S 13(tm) Mark Edwards/P, (tm, inset) Wave RF/P, (tl) Anna Kaminska/S, (bm) Martin Harvey/Corbis, (bm, inset) Babak Tafreshi/SPL 14(t, bg) Michael D Brown/S, (b, bg) Len Green/S, (tl) dimitris_k/S, (tr) Gunnar Pippel/S, (cl) nuttakit/S, (c) Bettmann/Corbis, (br) S, (bl) Roman Sigaev/S 15(tg) DiverS-photo/S, (tl) The Art Gallery Collection/Alamy, (tl, b) Marilyn Volan/S, (symbol c) Petr Vaclavek/S, (cr) Ambrophoto/S, (bl) Toponium/S, (br) Newspix/RF 16–7(bg) Steve Estvanik/S, (book) Valentin Agapov/S 16(t) gualtiero boffi/S, (c) George Steinmetz/Corbis, (c, bg) bartzuza/S, (bl) GI for Red Bull/GI, (br) Alexey Khromushin/F 17(t) Arcticphoto/Alamy, (c) Karen Kasmauski/Corbis, (b) Bloomberg via GI 18(l) Günter Flegar/P, (tr) AFP/GI, (br) Corbis

19(tl) Seleznev Oleg/S, (tr) KPA/Zuma/RF, (bl) Nik Wheeler/Corbis, (br) Sipa Press/RF 20–1(bg) nubephoto/S 20(l) SINOPIX/RF, (tr) Riou/Corbis, (br) Tim Hill/P 21(t) Envision/Corbis, (c) Mariana Bazo/Reuters/Corbis, (b) Ted Mead/P 22(t) Mike Keating/Newspix/RF, (b) Barcroft Media via GI 23(t) Alaska Stock Images/P, (cl) Alexis Rosenfeld/SPL, (bubble bg) fuyu liu/S, (b) NASA/SPL, (metal frame) Shawn Hine/S 24–5(bg) Molodec/S, (measurement instrument set) Leremy/S, (c) Natchapon L./S
24(bl) Superstock Inc/P 25(t) Factoria Singular/P, (b) Javier Larrea/P 26–7(bg) Andrey Burmakin/S, (science doodles) Lorelyn Medina/S, (b) Max Baumann/S 26(blue bg) Alexey Khromushin/F, (l) S, (tr) Jakub Krechowicz/S, (br) Sheila Terry/SPL 27(t) Bettmann/Corbis, (bl) Time & Life Pictures/GI, (br) hfng/S 28–9(m) John Van Hasselt/Sygma/Corbis
28(b) Bettmann/Corbis 29(tl) Sam Rosewarne/Newspix/RF, (tr) Reuters/Corbis, (b) Keith Ducatel 30(bg) Pallaske Pallaske/P, (t) R-studio/S, (t, b) Kompaniets Taras/S, (c) Luciano Mortula/S, (c, frame) kak2s/S, (b) Sukree Sukplang/X90021/Reuters/Corbis 31(m) JTB Photo/P, (t) Per-Andre Hoffmann/P, (frame) SuriyaPhoto/S 32–3(m) François Pugnet/Kipa/Corbis 32(t) RF, (c) Marco Beierer/S, (b) Kazela/S 33(t) Ian Salas/epa/Corbis 34(l) Valdrin Xhemaj/epa/Corbis, (tc) 2010 GI, (bc) Christian Kober/P, (r) imagebroker RF/P 35(tl) Sipa Press/RF, (tr) Charles & Josette Lenars/Corbis, (c) Zdorov Kirill Vladimirovich/S, (bl) Bildagentur RM/P, (br) GI 36–7(m) Alastair Muir/RF 36(b) Bildarchiv Monheim GmbH/Alamy, (parcel) Oliver Hoffmann/S 37(tl) GI, (cl) markrhiggins/S, (bl) Richcat/S, (r) Ray Tang/RF 38(t) AFP/GI, (b) Zhang Chuanqi/XinHua/Xinhua Press/Corbis 39(t) Jeff J Mitchell/Reuters/Corbis, (bl) Victor Fraile/Reuters/Corbis, (br) PILart/S

All other photographs are from: Corel, digitalSTOCK, digitalvision, Dreamstime.com, Fotolia.com, iStockphoto.com, John Foxx, PhotoAlto, PhotoDisc, PhotoEssentials, PhotoPro, Stockbyte

Every effort has been made to acknowledge the source and copyright holder of each picture. The publishers apologise for any unintentional errors or omissions.

SUPER HUMANS

Philip Steele
Consultant: Stewart Ross

Miles Kelly

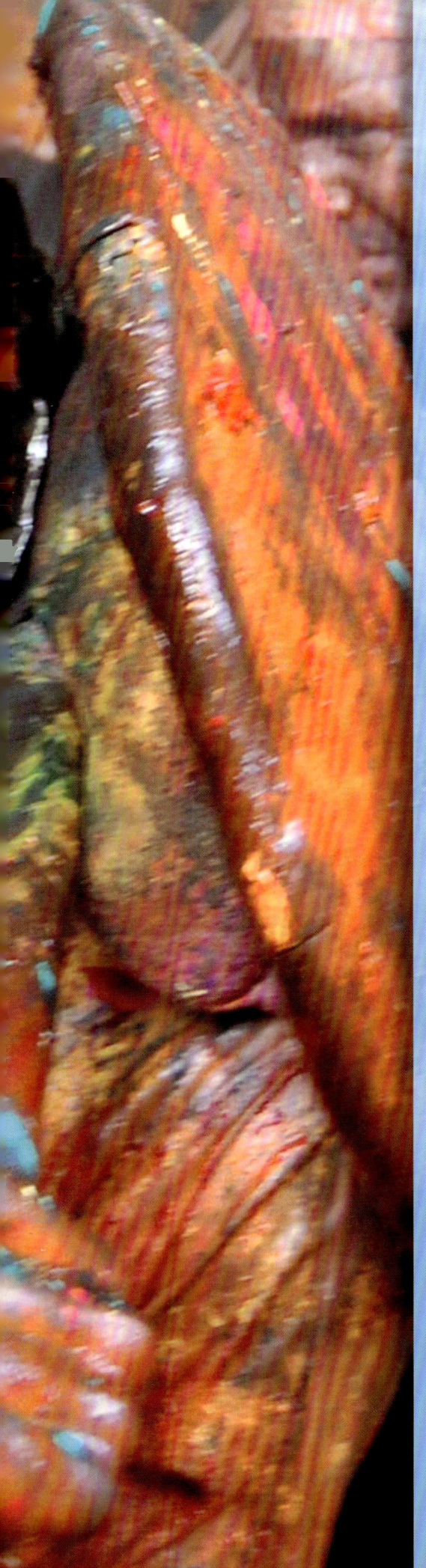

CONTENTS

The Amazing Human Body	6
The Things We Can Do	8
People, People Everywhere	10
Survival Around the World	12
Big Words and Crazy Numbers	14
Extreme Cities	16
No Place Like Home	18
Enjoy Your Meal	20
Ultimate Jobs	22
Awesome Architecture	24
Brilliant Brain Waves	26
Going the Distance	28
Millions of Pilgrims	30
Lives on the Line	32
Looking Good	34
The Art of Performing	36
Fun, Fun, Fun!	38
Index	40

◀ At Barsana, India, paint battles are all part of the fun before the Hindu spring festival of Holi.

The Amazing HUMAN BODY

The human body is built to survive. Babies are small and weak at birth, but as they grow they can expect to develop tough bones and powerful muscles. Humans can run at speed, jump high or jump long, swim underwater, carry heavy loads, and climb sheer rock faces. We are magnificent machines.

Adrenaline rush!
Bodies have an emergency mechanism that kicks in to deal with dangerous situations. A gland pumps a chemical messenger called adrenaline into the body. This increases oxygen in the blood and sends it to the muscles, which enables them to work harder. Fight or flight, the body is now ready to shift, really fast.

▼ *Bon anniversaire* Jeanne Calment! Or happy birthday to the oldest-ever woman, here celebrating her 122nd birthday.

How fast can we go?
Like a bolt of lightning! In 2009, Jamaican athlete Usain Bolt ran the 100 m in 9.58 seconds and the 200 m in 19.19 seconds. Back in 1988 the late "Flo-Jo" (Florence Griffith-Joyner) ran the 100 m in 10.49 seconds and the 200 m in 21.34 seconds.

▲ Maximum power! Usain Bolt sprints the 100 m in 2010. He holds World and Olympic records for the 100 m, 200 m, and 4 x 100 m relay.

How long can we live?
On average, humans can expect to live for 66.12 years. In Macau, China, life expectancy is as high as 84.36 years. Tragically, in Angola, Africa, it is only 38.2 years. The greatest age known to have been reached by a woman is 122 years and 164 days, by Jeanne Calment of France (1875–1997). The oldest-ever man was Shigechiyo Izumi of Japan (1865–1986), who reached 120 years and 237 days.

During an average lifetime you may: Walk 13,700 mi (22,000 km)... Produce 200 billion new red blood cells every day...

How strong can we get?

Olympic weightlifters take part in two events called the "snatch" (from squat to overhead) and the "clean and jerk" (from floor to shoulders, then an overhead push). Between 2002 and 2003, Iranian strongman Hossein Rezazadeh managed a 469-lb (213-kg) snatch, a 581-lb (263.5-kg) clean and jerk, and a total load of 1,041 lb (472 kg). Between 2008 and 2009, women's champion Jang Mi-ran of South Korea smashed the records with 309 lb (140 kg), 412 lb (187 kg), and a total of 719 lb (326 kg).

▼ Muscles bulge as Hossein Rezazadeh gets a grip. His nickname? The "Iranian Hercules."

▶ By the age of 22, Robert Wadlow measured 8ft 11.1 in (2.72 m).

THE HUMAN BODY HAS MORE THAN 620 MUSCLES. THE BIGGEST, THE GLUTEUS MAXIMUS, COVERS THE BUTTOCKS.

Tall and short

The tallest known human in history was an American called Robert Wadlow (1918–1940), nicknamed the "Giant of Illinois." The shortest man living in the world today is Khagendra Thapa Magar (b. 1992), from Nepal.

▶ Khagendra Thapa Magar is just 2 ft 2.5 in (0.6 m) tall.

THERE ARE 206 BONES IN THE ADULT HUMAN BODY. A BABY HAS MORE THAN 300, BUT SOME OF THESE SOON FUSE TOGETHER.

Spend 12 years talking... Drink 100,000 pt (50,000 l) of liquid... Blink 415 million times... Grow 60 mi (90 km) of hair on your head...

The Things WE CAN DO

The human body can survive in all sorts of environments, but it does have physical limits. At high altitudes mountaineers may require extra supplies of oxygen. Extreme cold may bring hypothermia and frostbite, while extreme heat can burn the skin and cause sunstroke. Even so, increasing numbers of people are pushing their bodies to the limit—with extreme sports and activities.

Ice climbing

Climbing a sheer rockface is a feat at any time, but climbing it when it is covered in thick ice is even more amazing. Ice climbers also tackle glaciers, icefalls, and frozen waterfalls using boot spikes (crampons), ropes, and ice axes to get a grip. All climbers need physical strength, stamina—and a keen sense of balance.

▲ Ice climbers need to keep a cool head. This extreme sport depends upon technique and skill. Ice can be very strong and can safely support ropes and spikes—if they are used correctly.

Super endurance

Every year, thousands of people take part in the Tough Guy competition in Perton, U.K. Participants face the ultimate stamina challenge, racing through water, mud, smoke, and ice in what is claimed to be the world's toughest test of strength and endurance.

◀ A would-be Tough Guy tackles a wall of flames. Many competitors don't finish the course.

▲ An exhilarating tandem dive. At competition level, skydiving requires supreme body control.

▶ A cliff diver leaps from La Quebrada clifftop, near Acapulco, Mexico. Sometimes people dive here by night, holding flaming torches.

Skydiving
After the jump from the aircraft you hurtle forward. For a mighty minute or so you go into glorious freefall as you drop. Then it's time for the parachute to open, and a gentle glide down to Earth. But a regular jump is not enough of a thrill for some—in 2006, 400 jumpers from 31 countries set a record for the largest formation freefall.

Taking the plunge
A 100-ft (30-m) dive into a narrow rocky cove near Acapulco in Mexico is a true test of nerves. These professional divers must avoid the cliff's deadly rocks and time their entry into the water—which is only 6–16 ft (2–5 m) deep—to perfection, while taking account of the waves.

Paralympic champions
The Paralympic Games are a major sporting competition for elite athletes with disabilities. Sports include swimming, judo, ice-sled hockey, tennis, shooting, and wheelchair basketball and rugby. They are just as competitive as the Olympic Games—around 4,000 athletes from nearly 150 countries participate.

▲ Long jump triumph for Germany's Wojtek Czyz. At the Beijing Paralympics in 2008, he leaped 21.3 ft (6.5 m) to claim the gold medal.

People, People EVERYWHERE

It is called a population explosion—the rapid growth of the number of people living on our planet to nearly **7 billion*** individuals. During the last **200 years** the world population has grown by about seven times, thanks to improvements in food production, water supply, healthcare, and medication. By **2050** the figure may have grown to about 12 billion—but we can only guess.

*6,914,369,936 and counting (world population estimate, April 2011).

The world's peoples live in **266** different nations, dependencies, and territories.

More than **5 BILLION** pizzas are eaten each year around the world.

1 IN 10 people live on less than U.S. $10 (£6) per day.

27 PERCENT of the people in the world are under 14 years of age.

About **1 IN 5** of the world's population is Chinese.

Over **60 PERCENT** of the world's population lives in the continent of Asia, while less than **ONE PERCENT** live in Oceania (including Australia).

How many languages are spoken in the world? Estimates vary, but about **6,800** might be a good guess.

The top 10 most densely populated lands include small territories, ministates, and islands with limited space. Top of these is the Chinese special region of **MACAU**, with 48,003 people per sq mi (18,534 per sq km).

On average, women live **3.78** years longer than men.

About **82 PERCENT** of adults in the world can read and write.

There are very slightly **MORE MEN** than women in the world.

Why do people talk so much? There are **5.3 BILLION** cellphones in the world, and **1.3 BILLION** landlines.

It has been estimated that for every single human on the planet there are **2 BILLION** insects.

267 babies are born every minute.

Traffic jam! There are about **128** motor vehicles for every 1000 humans in the world.

Every year, passengers make **3.2 BILLION** journeys on the Tokyo subway system in Japan.

About **15 MILLION** people worldwide are refugees, uprooted from their homes by disasters such as persecution, war, or famine.

Rice provides more than **20 PERCENT** of all the calories that humans consume around the world.

The loneliest independent nation is Mongolia. Its vast deserts and grasslands have only **4.4 PEOPLE PER SQ MI** (1.7 per sq km).

People over the age of **65** account for **7.6** percent of the world population.

The territory with the **LOWEST POPULATION GROWTH RATE** is the Northern Marianas Islands, in the Pacific Ocean, with a figure of **-7.8 PERCENT.**

1 IN 8 people in the world have no access to safe water supplies.

In the next minute, **133 passengers** will arrive or depart from London's Heathrow Airport in the U.K., one of the busiest airports in the world.

Humans only live on the **29.1** percent of Earth's surface that is dry land.

The population of China is estimated at **1,336,718,015.** Closing the gap is neighboring India with 1,189,172,906. India has a higher growth rate than China, which it is expected to overtake by 2040.

The world's continents have an overall population density of **119** per sq mi (46 per sq km).

Burundi in Africa and the United Arab Emirates in the Middle East both have the highest population growth rate, with an annual increase of **3.69** percent.

The Indian government's 2010 census is claimed to be the largest ever undertaken. It employed **2.5 MILLION** officials, cost $1.4 billion (£875 million), and created 13,000 tons of paperwork.

The most densely populated large country is Bangladesh, with **2,919** people per sq mi (1,126 per sq km).

The world's most sparsely populated territory is Arctic Greenland, with only **0.025** people per sq mi (0.067 per sq km).

The average age of a human being alive today is **28.4** years.

1 IN 8 people in the world are malnourished.

How many people have **ever lived** on Earth? It's very hard to say, but some experts have estimated a figure of about **115 BILLION.**

Icy **ANTARCTICA** is a continent with no permanent population. With the thousand or so international scientists based there, the population density is only about **0.00003** per sq mi (0.00007 per sq km).

11

SURVIVAL
Around the World

Over hundreds of thousands of years, the human body has adapted to cope in all sorts of environments and climates. Modern city dwellers may no longer have to battle with the forces of nature every day, but many peoples around the world still struggle to survive in very hostile conditions.

THE SAAMI PEOPLE OF ARCTIC SWEDEN, NORWAY, FINLAND, AND RUSSIA USE A TENT CALLED A LAVVU AS A SHELTER WHEN HERDING REINDEER. IT WAS TRADITIONALLY MADE OF REINDEER HIDE SUPPORTED ON POLES.

▶ The Inuit from Ellesmere Island in Nunavut, Canada, wrap up warm to withstand the icy conditions of their homeland. Grabbing his harpoon, this Arctic hunter jumps from one ice floe to another in search of food.

▶ The Inuit can survive when hunting by building a shelter or *igdlu* from frozen blocks of snow.

The ice people
In the icy wilderness of northwest Greenland the temperature may drop to −40°F (−40°C) in winter, and during this season the Sun does not rise for 14 weeks. A nice summer day might reach 32°F (0°C)! This region is home to the most northerly native people in the world. They form a small community called the Inughuit, or Polar Eskimos. Only about 1,000 people speak their language, Inuktun. The Inughuit travel by dog sled and live by hunting walrus and fishing.

THE ABORIGINES OF AUSTRALIA'S DESERTS AND ARID SCRUBLAND HAVE LEARNED HOW TO OBTAIN WATER FROM TREE ROOTS, LEAVES, AND ROCK HOLLOWS.

Deep in the forest

The Yanomamo people of the Amazon rain forest in South America are experts in forest survival. They hunt animals with poisoned arrows, gather grubs, and grow plants. The population is declining because their lands in Brazil have been invaded by gold miners, who have brought in diseases to which the Yanomamo have no resistance.

◀ Dense rain forest may be a barrier to the outside world, but it provides food and shelter to the humans who live there.

▶ A view from a helicopter shows a Yanomamo village in perfect isolation, deep in the forest.

Desert survivors

In North Africa's Sahara Desert, temperatures may soar above 122°F (50°C). The only places where people can settle are around oases, or water holes. The Tuareg people are camel herders and traders. They are nomads who travel along ancient trade routes across the desert. Tuareg men traditionally wear black turbans and wrap their faces in dark blue scarves or veils.

▶ Desert survival depends on camels. They can carry a half-ton load for 25 mi (40 km) a day—and go for a week without water.

▼ Tuareg traders break for the night in the Algerian Sahara. Once the Sun goes down, the fierce heat of the day gives way to below freezing temperatures.

BIG WORDS & CRAZY NUMBERS

Talking, counting, and calculating are some of the key skills behind our success as human beings. They make it possible for us to teach and learn, to work out how to do things, and organize ourselves. The first forms of writing words and numbering appeared in Asia more than 5,000 years ago.

Alphabetti spaghetti
The 26-letter alphabet for the English language is quite a modest one. The world's longest alphabet is that of the Khmer language, used in Cambodia in Southeast Asia. It has 74 letters. The shortest is the Rotokas alphabet, used by about 4,000 people on the island of Bougainville in Papua New Guinea. It has just 11 letters.

◀ The teachings of Kong Fuzi, or Confucius (551–479 BC), were a key part of education in ancient China, and are still studied today.

Do you speak global?
Standard Chinese or "Mandarin" is spoken by about 845 million people as a first language. The number for Spanish is 329 million and for English is 328 million. Many millions speak English as a second language, and it is spoken in more countries than any other—112.

A language of symbols
The Chinese language does not use an alphabet, but symbols called characters. It traditionally has about 47,035 of them, but for everyday use between 3,000 and 4,000 is sufficient.

▼ A railway station sign for a town in Wales that bears the longest name of any place in Britain.

LLANFAIRPWLLGWYNGYLLGOGERYCHWYRNDROBWLLLLANTYSILIOGOGOGOCH
Llan-vire-pooll-guin-gill-go-ger-u-queern-drob-ooll-llandus-ilio-gogo-goch

THE COUNTRY WITH THE HIGHEST NUMBER OF LANGUAGES IS PAPUA NEW GUINEA, WITH 820.

POLONIUS: What do you read, my lord?

HAMLET: Words, words, words.
Hamlet Act II, Scene II

Shakespeare
The genius William Shakespeare (1564–1616) is probably the best-known playwright of all time. His 38 plays contain 884,429 words, spoken by 1,221 characters.

14

How big is Earth?

The circumference of our planet at the Equator (the imaginary circle that runs around the center of Earth) is 24,901.8 mi (40,075.6 km). Ancient Greek mathematician Eratosthenes of Cyrene (276–195 BC) calculated it at 252,000 *stadia*, which is thought to have equaled 24,660 mi (39,690 km). If this is the case, Eratosthenes was only one percent off—not a bad effort, in the days before calculators and satellites!

ERATOSTHENES

"CLICK" SOUNDS FORM AN IMPORTANT PART OF SPOKEN LANGUAGE IN SOME AREAS OF SOUTHERN AFRICA.

THE LANGUAGE OF SILBO, FROM THE CANARY ISLANDS, USES PENETRATING WHISTLES THAT CAN BE HEARD OVER VERY LONG DISTANCES.

Early methods of counting were based on people's fingers and toes, which is why most people today use a decimal counting system—one that is based on the number ten. The ancient Babylonians based their counting system on units of 60, which is why we still have 60 minutes in one hour and 360 degrees in a full circle.

Crunching numbers

The Greek letter *pi* is a handy little symbol. It is written as π and it helps you work out the area of a circle or its circumference. The value of π = 3.1415926535... and so on, and so on. For how long? π has actually been calculated to more than a trillion decimal places!

In 2007, 16-year-old Australian student Peter Thamm recited pi to more than 10,000 decimal places. The current record-holder is Chinese student Lu Chao, who managed an incredible 67,890 decimal places.

Extreme CITIES

People usually build cities in an ideal spot with good supplies of food and water, deep harbors, good road and rail links, and a healthy climate. But sometimes cities have to be located in remote areas or difficult terrain, or where weather conditions are extreme.

On top of the world

La Paz is the highest capital in the world. It is the administrative center of Bolivia, sited amid the peaks of the Andes mountains. It has merged with the neighboring city of El Alto, so the total built-up area has altitudes of 9,800–13,600 ft (3,000–4,150 m) above sea level. Locals have adapted to living at high altitude, but visitors may suffer from severe headaches and sickness until they become acclimatized to low levels of oxygen.

Onward and upward— La Paz is still climbing up the mountainside.

La Paz boasts the world's highest velodrome, which has been used by cycling champions Arnaud Tournant of France and Sir Chris Hoy of Scotland to complete record-breaking one-kilometer time trials. The thin air is less resistant, but with less oxygen the body must work harder.

THE WORLD'S LOWEST CITY IS ALSO ONE OF THE OLDEST. JERICHO OR ARIHA IN PALESTINE IS 846 FT (258 M) BELOW SEA LEVEL, AND HAS STOOD THROUGH 11,000 YEARS OF HUMAN HISTORY.

Hot-hot-hot spots

The hottest temperature ever recorded on Earth was in 1922 in the city of Al 'Aziziyah in Libya, when the thermometer shot up to 135.9°F (57.7°C). Cities with exceptionally hot periods of the year include Kuwait City in Kuwait, and Ahvaz in Iran. Both have months where the average maximum temperature reaches 115°F (46°C).

~Post Card~

The big fridge

Which is the coldest city on Earth? Yakutsk, in Siberia, is built on soil that remains permanently frozen, even in summer. In winter, temperatures can average −40°F (−40°C) and may drop below −50°F (−60°C), which is cold enough for people's glasses to freeze to their faces!

In most cities, a small leak in a water pipe means a small puddle. In Yakutsk, Siberia, it can mean one giant iceberg!

Monster metropolis

A global movement is taking place, as people all over the world move from the countryside into cities in search of work and a better life. Cities are massive consumers of power and water and produce mountains of waste and refuse.

OVER HALF OF THE WORLD'S POPULATION NOW LIVE IN CITIES.

Tokyo's Shinjuku district is a vast sprawl of offices and very busy people.

A DAY IN THE BIG APPLE

New York City is home to 2.7 percent of the U.S. population. Every day, New Yorkers…

* Use more than one billion gal (3.8 billion l) of water.
* Throw away enough garbage to fill the Empire State Building to the top floor.
* Make about five million trips on the subway.
* Are employed in 3.7 million jobs citywide.

Megacities and megaregions

Japan's capital Tokyo has grown so huge that it has merged with nearby cities such as Yokohama, Chiba, and Kawasaki. The joint urban area, or "conurbation," is home to about 35.7 million people.

On the south coast of China, conurbations have merged to create the most urban region on the planet, taking in cities such as Guangzhou, Shenzhen, and Hong Kong, with a population of about 120 million.

The most crowded city on Earth is Mumbai in India, with about 47,572 people per sq mi (29,560 per sq km).

No Place LIKE HOME

Many modern towns and cities look much the same wherever the location. But some people still live in traditional or unusual homes, where design is determined by climate and landscape, by available building materials, or by way of life.

HOLE IN THE GROUND
Coober Pedy, Australia

To escape the heat of the Sun, the first opal miners often made their homes by converting disused mining shafts into living spaces. They were soon excavating new homes from the rock—they called them dugouts. Dugouts may include several bedrooms and spacious living rooms—all of them naturally air-conditioned!

CAVE DWELLINGS
Cappadocia, Turkey

In this area of exceptional natural wonders, the landscape is made up of volcanic rocks, which have been eroded into unusual pillars, columns, and caves. For thousands of years, local people have carved out homes, storerooms, and churches from the soft rock. The caves were often used as places of refuge when invading armies swept across the land. Today some have been made into hotels for tourists.

LUXURY HOUSEBOAT
Kashmir, India

Houseboats are used in many parts of the world. Some of the most beautiful and decorative houseboats are moored around the lakes of Kashmir. Houseboats also line some of the canals of Amsterdam in the Netherlands, and provide homes for fishing families around Hong Kong's famous harbors.

TAKE TEA IN MY TENT
Eurasion steppes

The tent is the ideal living place for nomads—people on the move. The *yurt* or *ger* of the Mongols and Turkic peoples of the Eurasian steppes are domes of felt cloth supported by willow poles. They are cool in summer but warm in the bitterly cold winter, heated by stoves.

▶ These Mongolian tents look surprisingly cozy and inviting, despite the snowy grassland surrounding them.

Middle Eastern deserts

The tents used by nomadic herders in the Sahara and Arabian deserts are made of woven wool and hair from camels or goats. They are supported by poles and long guy ropes, and pitched low to provide a minimum of resistance to wind and sandstorms.

◀ This tent offers home comforts in the middle of the Moroccan Sahara.

FLOATING REED HOUSES
Southern Iraq

The Ma'dan or Marsh Arabs live in the wetlands of southern Iraq. Their traditional homes are built from reeds and sited on riverbanks or on artificial islands, made of mud and bundles of reeds. The people have suffered greatly from warfare and the draining of the marshes. Only now is the water beginning to flow once again through this landscape.

▼ For the Ma'dan, the wetlands provide natural resources, and act as a highway.

Enjoy Your Meal

An old saying goes: "One man's meat is another man's poison." We don't all enjoy the same kinds of food. Often the meals we were brought up on seem the safest and tastiest to us, while the dishes eaten by people in countries other than our own may seem strange, or even downright disgusting. But go on—be adventurous!

Frogs' Legs — France

In parts of France, frogs' legs are eaten, fried in breadcrumbs. It's said that they taste a lot like chicken wings, and it's not just a French thing—they're also popular in the U.S. state of Louisiana and in China. And if you find yourself in Indonesia you might try *swikee*—a delicious frogs' legs soup.

Fugu — Japan

Would you have the stomach to eat a fish dish that could kill you—even for a dare? One Japanese delicacy is fugu, or pufferfish, and some parts of this strange animal contain a deadly poison. Only specially trained chefs know how to prepare the meal so that it can be eaten safely. And accidents do happen...

Haggis — Scotland

First you need a sheep. Chop up its lungs, heart, and liver and mix with oatmeal, suet, and onion. Then cook for three hours—once you've packed it all into a sheep's intestine. On January 25 each year, Scots honor their national poet, Robert Burns, by playing bagpipes and reciting a poem to the haggis before digging in.

Birds' Nest Soup — China

Don't worry—you don't actually have to swallow sticks and mud! This soup is an expensive delicacy made from the edible saliva of cave swiftlet birds. The birds use the saliva to build their nests in the caves of Borneo, or in special nesting houses where it can be harvested.

Also on the global menu...

Dog — *Vietnam*
The original hot dog? Dogs are eaten in many parts of east Asia.

Donkey Salami — *Italy*
Most Italian salami is made of pork but donkey, horse, and goat are also used.

Sheep's Eyes — *Arabia*
A whole roast sheep may be served at an Arabian feast, including—as a real treat—the eyeballs.

Iguana — *South America*
Stewed or roast iguana (a type of large lizard) is a traditional food in parts of Central America.

Locust — *North Africa*
Desert locusts are big grasshoppers. Perfectly bite-sized, they can be fried, roasted, boiled, and even sundried.

Alligator — *USA*
These huge reptiles have always been eaten in the southern states. Now scarce in the wild, they are farmed for their hides and meat.

Guinea Pig — Peru

Guinea pigs provide a really popular meal in Peru and in some other regions of the Andes mountains. These small, furry creatures can be raised in the home or bought at street markets, for frying or roasting. The meat is said to be low in fat and full of goodness.

Witchetty Grub — Australia

Yummy! These large larvae can be eaten raw or baked in hot ashes. The grubs are a traditional favorite of Australia's Aborigines. Other "bush tucker" (wild food) has become popular in restaurants—including kangaroo, emu, and goanna (lizard) meat.

21

Ultimate JOBS

Most people are only too happy to do jobs that do not require high-risk action. Others would not be at all content sitting at a computer all day or working in a store. They prefer putting themselves on the line!

Daredevils

Who's that leaping from a burning car in the movie? The starring actor? More likely it's a stunt double—someone who looks similar at a distance, but is able to perform extraordinary feats of acrobatics, balance, or endurance. Of course, many of the extreme scenes we see on screen involve trick photography, computer-generated imagery, and special effects, but there are still people whose daily grind might involve performing a metal-crashing, rubber-burning car chase to perfection.

◀ Flaming French stuntman Nicolas Saurey takes a dive— luckily, into a pool of water!

A head for heights

The job of a steeplejack is to carry out high-level repair, maintenance, or demolition of very tall structures such as church steeples, bell towers, factory chimneys, or industrial towers. Steeplejacks have to erect ladders, use ropes, abseil, or be suspended in cradles from wires. Window cleaners may have to work from cradles high on the sides of skyscrapers, while bridge builders may have to reel steel cable at the top of a suspension bridge, hundreds of feet above a river. Modern high-level workers use safety harnesses, ropes, and hardhats. Even so, it's still pretty scary!

◀ Don't look down! These intrepid workers are cleaning the helipad on the 1,053-ft- (321-m-) high Burj el Arab hotel in Dubai.

ACTOR SÉBASTIEN FOUCAN (CASINO ROYALE, 2006) COFOUNDED THE SPORT OF FREERUNNING— NEGOTIATING THE OBSTACLES OF CITY STRUCTURES WITH VAULTS, SPINS, AND ACROBATICS.

22

All hands on deck
One of the most dangerous professions in the U.S. is crab fishing. Working for long hours on a trawler in freezing seas, with giant waves, gales, a slippery deck, nets, winches, rocks, and reefs can be a high-risk way to earn a living.

◀ Bringing in the catch is a feat of endurance for these fishermen.

Diving to great depths
Divers need to venture into very deep water for all sorts of reasons, including scientific research, archeology, geology, and industrial monitoring. One big problem is water pressure, which can damage the human body and cause a sickness called the "bends." An atmospheric diving suit or ADS allows a diver to go down to extreme depths—a maximum of 2,300 ft (700 m)—in safety. It is like a suit of armor, made of aluminum or special plastic.

▲ Wearing a "newtsuit" (a type of ADS) allows this rescue diver to descend to depths greater than 820 ft (250 m).

▶ Astronauts are weightless as they work far above Earth—and the view is spectacular!

Space walkers
An astronaut's job is literally out of this world. When leaving the spacecraft for extravehicular activity (EVA), he or she may be floating in space perhaps 220 mi (350 km) above our planet, often trying at the same time to fix a broken piece of equipment or carry out an experiment. The astronaut may be tethered to the spacecraft with an oxygen line, or be self-sufficient with a personal mobile maneuvering unit (MMU).

Awesome ARCHITECTURE

Humans have come a long way since they built the first simple huts from twigs and grass. Today we can design fantastic structures, made of a huge range of materials from steel and glass to concrete and plastic. Modern buildings can dazzle and deceive the eye, soar into the sky—or do the most amazingly clever things!

BIRD'S NEST STADIUM
This incredible tangle of steel is actually the National Stadium in the Chinese capital city, Beijing. It was built for the spectacular 2008 Olympic Games. Future use will include a shopping mall development.

BEIJING, CHINA

CORNWALL, ENGLAND

EDEN PROJECT
These domes of plastic and steel wouldn't look out of place in a science fiction landscape, but instead they bubble up from the green fields of Cornwall, England. Each dome contains its own mini-environment or biome. Featuring the world's largest indoor rain forest, global allotments, and Mediterranean blossoms, all kinds of plant life thrive here.

ODEILLO, FRANCE

EXPOSITION
Le soleil apprivoisé

SOLAR FURNACE
The giant mirrors at Odeillo, France, reflect the rays of the Sun onto a larger, curved mirror (shown here). The focused reflections create a single point where the temperature can reach up to 6,330°F (3,500°C), which can then be used for industrial purposes such as generating electricity and melting steel.

ROTTERDAM, NETHERLANDS

CUBE HOUSES
It looks a bit like massive children's playing blocks have tumbled across the square. Completed in 1984, these buildings are in fact a mini village of three-story houses in Rotterdam in the Netherlands, which were designed by Dutch architect Piet Blom to tilt at an angle of 45 degrees.

25

Brilliant BRAIN WAVES

Throughout history people have made great discoveries and come up with fantastic inventions to transform the way we live. Where would we be today without the wheel, or writing (both invented in ancient Iraq 5,000–6,000 years ago)? Or indeed more trivial inventions such as chewing gum (used in Stone Age Finland about 5,000 years ago)? Inventors are still working away today, to come up with new ideas for the 21st century.

Leonardo da Vinci

The greatest inventor of all time

Italian artist Leonardo da Vinci (1452–1519) had some of the best ideas for inventions long before their time, including helicopters, hang gliders, crank mechanisms, weapons, portable bridges, and a musical instrument called the viola organista, which was the first bowed keyboard instrument ever devised.

Da Vinci's helicopter concept was based on a child's toy.

Da Vinci's 1478 design for a self-propelled car.

5 PRETTY USELESS (IF NOT DOWNRIGHT WACKY) INVENTIONS

* Clockwork weights to drop on your head and wake you up (1882)
* Eagle-powered balloon (1887)
* Automatic hat-raiser (1896)
* Obstacle courses for goldfish (2009)
* Electric ear dryer (2009)

Deadly discovery

Invented in China about 1,200 years ago, gunpowder is arguably the most deadly invention ever. In World War I (1914–1918) alone, 9.7 million soldiers were killed worldwide, and 8.9 million civilians—many the victims of shells, rifle and machine gun fire, and bombs.

Terror strikes a World War I battlefield... gunpowder was a brilliant brain wave with terrible consequences.

ALEXANDER FLEMING DISCOVERED (BY ACCIDENT) THAT PENICILLIUM MOLD, FOUND ON STALE BREAD, COULD FIGHT DEADLY BACTERIA. THE ANTIBIOTIC WONDER DRUG PENICILLIN WAS BEING PRODUCED IN THE U.S. BY 1943.

Lifesaving science

Antibiotics are one of the most useful inventions of all time. These modern drugs have saved many millions of lives around the world. The credit is due to many scientists of the 19th and 20th centuries, including Louis Pasteur, Robert Koch, John Tyndall, Paul Ehrlich, Alexander Fleming, Gerhard Domagk, René Dubos, Howard Florey, and Ernst Chain.

Discovered: the secret of life

Genetics is one of the most important modern sciences. During the 1860s, Austrian botanist Gregor Mendel worked out the laws of inheritance—how living things pass on their characteristics down the generations. In 1869 it was discovered that cells contain a hereditary material called deoxyribonucleic acid—or "DNA." Scientists who tried to determine the structure of this chemical included Rosalind Franklin and Maurice Wilson, and in 1953 the code was finally cracked by James Watson and Francis Crick, providing a springboard for 21st-century science and medicine.

Gregor Mendel

HOW WE GOT ONLINE...

1834 First attempt at a mechanical computer by British inventor Charles Babbage

1946 First electronic computer, the 30-ton ENIAC, designed and built at the University of Pennsylvania, U.S.

1971 First single silicon chip microprocessor (U.S.)

1975 First home computer (U.S.)

1973-80s Development of e-mail

1989 Proposal for a World Wide Web by British computer scientist Tim Berners-Lee

2000 First broadband access to the Internet

2006 Rise of social networking sites

Going the DISTANCE

Travelers have always pushed into the unknown, crossing deserts, hacking their way through jungles, or sailing the seven seas. Today we can travel around the world in comfort, but some people still prefer to do it the hard way—and even relish the challenge.

◂ Exhausted but victorious, French climber and explorer Laurence de la Ferrière successfully reaches the South Pole.

Into the deep freeze

Frenchwoman Laurence de la Ferrière has climbed Himalayan peaks, explored the ice floes of the Bering Strait, made a solo crossing of Greenland, traversed the whole range of the Alps, and made a two-stage solo crossing of Antarctica (1996–1997 and 1999–2000).

Ultimate journey

The first expedition to the South Pole was led by Norwegian explorer Roald Amundsen, and arrived on December 14, 1911. On January 17, 1912, a British team led by Robert Falcon Scott also reached the Pole—"Great God!" Scott wrote in his diary, "This is an awful place." On the return journey, Scott and his whole team perished in appalling conditions.

Members of Captain Scott's ill-fated expedition to the South Pole.

THE LOWEST TEMPERATURE EVER RECORDED AT THE SOUTH POLE IS A DECIDEDLY CHILLY -117°F (-82.8°C)!

▼ Jessica Watson takes the helm of her yacht, *Pink Lady*. She was declared Young Australian of the Year for 2011.

Up, up, and away
Steve Fossett (1944–2007) was an aviator, sailor, skier, and climber. In 2002 he became the first man to fly solo around the world in a balloon, without stopping. His flight from Australia covered 20,626 mi (33,195 km).

◀ Fossett's balloon, *Solo Spirit*, leaves the east coast of Australia behind and heads out over the open ocean.

Going solo
In 2009–2010, Australian yachtswoman Jessica Watson sailed solo around the world. Although her route from Sydney across the Pacific, Atlantic, and Indian oceans was not the official one, it was an incredible achievement. At the time she was just 16 years old.

Downriver
Does anyone fancy going for a stroll? There probably wouldn't be many volunteers if the stroll in question takes 860 days and is about 4,000 mi (about 6,400 km) long. This was the achievement of English explorer Ed Stafford. He followed the course of the mighty Amazon River from its source to the ocean, completing his trek in 2010.

◀ Ed Stafford and his companion "Cho" Sanchez Rivera trekked through swamps and dense forest—home to many potentially lethal creatures including jaguars, piranha, and killer bees.

Millions of Pilgrims

Some of the world's largest gatherings of people, biggest buildings, and most spectacular events are associated with religious belief and worship. The majority of the people in the world follow faiths, which may vary from traditional spirit beliefs to large, organized religions. More than one billion people around the world do not follow a religion or are nonbelievers.

THE GOLDEN TEMPLE OF THE SIKHS, IN AMRITSAR, INDIA, IS A SITE OF GREAT BEAUTY.

▲ Seville's great altarpiece shows 45 scenes from the life of Christ.

Golden glory

Some of the world's most spectacular religious buildings are built to sparkle! The altarpiece of the Christian Seville Cathedral in Spain, one of the biggest in the world, is covered in gold, and was the life's work of a single craftsman—Flemish sculptor Pieter Dancart.

The Harmandir Sahib, or Golden Temple, was built between 1585 and 1604 at Amritsar in India. It is the center of the Sikh faith and its gold roof and walls are reflected in the still waters of an artificial lake.

The Buddhist Shwedagon pagoda in Yangon, Burma, is plated in gold donated by the faithful. The crown at the top contains an incredible 5,448 diamonds and 2,317 rubies.

◀ Shwedagon attracts Buddhist pilgrims from all over Burma.

Christian Trappist monks speak only rarely, as they believe speech can be a distraction from thought and prayer.

Jain monks may wear masks out of reverence for all forms of life, in case they accidentally swallow a fly or inhale a microbe.

THE BIGGEST STATUE OF THE BUDDHA IS AT LESHAN IN CHINA AND IS 233 FT (71 M) HIGH. IT WAS CARVED FROM THE CLIFF FACE BETWEEN AD 713 AND 803.

THE DRAMATIC LIGHTS OF ESALA PERAHERA, CELEBRATED BY SRI LANKAN BUDDHISTS.

Many, many people...

The world's biggest annual pilgrimage is the Hajj, the journey to Mecca in Saudi Arabia by more than two million Muslims every year. Pilgrimage is one of the basic "pillars" or duties of the Islamic faith, and the mosque at Mecca is the largest in the world.

The world's biggest religious gatherings are a series of Hindu pilgrimages held in northern India over cycles of four, six, 12, and 144 years. The biggest ever of these was a Maha Kumbh Mela at Allahabad in northern India in 2001, which may have attracted as many as 60 million people.

▼ Muslim pilgrims at Mecca must walk seven times around the Kaaba, a sacred structure covered in black silk.

All lit up

One of the most spectacular religious processions is the Esala Perahera, organized by Buddhist monks in Kandy, Sri Lanka. It honors a sacred relic, the Buddha's tooth. Elephants take part dressed in spectacular cloth that is decorated with electric lightbulbs, and there are flags, musicians, drummers, glittering costumes, cracking whips, flaming torches, and peacock dancers.

In Turkey, mystics of the Sufi Mevlevi order perform a religious dance, which involves spinning round and round. They are known as "whirling dervishes."

On Jewish religious days such as Rosh Hashanah and Yom Kippur, a Tokea blows the sacred shofar—a ram's horn trumpet.

31

Lives on the LINE

The worst events often bring out the best in people. When there is an accident or emergency, ambulance crews, police, or firefighters are soon at the scene, helping out and saving lives. When there is a major natural or man-made disaster, people often show heroism in extremely difficult conditions, putting their own lives on the line to save others.

Lifeboat SOS!

No one chooses to go to sea during an extreme storm—unless there are lives to save. Towering waves, gale-force winds, blizzards, injured crew, loose cargo, and foundering ships may all be encountered on callouts. Helicopters may also be required to lower lines to stricken vessels in dangerous weather conditions or poor visibility.

In the U.K., search-and-rescue lifeboats are operated by volunteers of the Royal National Lifeboat Institution (RNLI). Since it was founded in 1824 this charity has saved more than 139,000 lives at sea. In 2009, RNLI crews were called out on 9,154 occasions and saved 8,186 people.

▲ An inshore lifeboat slams into the waves as a crew goes into action off the coast of Wales, U.K.

Fighting the blaze

Fires may break out naturally in hot, dry weather or when lightning strikes. Most fires are the result of human error—for example gas explosions or house fires. Firefighters are in the front line, directing water hoses, entering burning buildings, demolishing structures, or clearing vegetation to prevent fire spreading. Firefighters also attend other emergency incidents, such as chemical spillages, road and rail crashes, and air disasters.

◀ Fighting a wall of fire needs bravery, physical strength, and clear thinking in the midst of a crisis.

A BURIED AVALANCHE VICTIM MAY HAVE JUST 20 MINUTES TO LIVE, BUT IF THEY ARE CARRYING A TRANSCEIVER (A DEVICE THAT CAN TRANSMIT AND SEND RADIO SIGNALS), A LOCATION SIGNAL CAN BE SENT TO RESCUERS.

▲ A rescue team calls in the helicopter to take an accident victim off the freezing mountainside, and away to the nearest hospital.

Precipice peril

Mountain search-and-rescue teams may be made up of full-time professionals, or volunteers. They often have to turn out in appalling conditions, and must know the terrain, and be experts at climbing, first aid, and communications. They may use dogs and probes to locate people buried in avalanches, and call in support from helicopter rescue services. Piloting helicopters in mountainous areas in poor conditions is a hazardous and highly skilled task.

UNDERGROUND SURVIVAL

On August 5, 2010, a tunnel at the San José gold and copper mine in Chile, caved in. For 69 days the world held its breath—33 miners were trapped about 2,300 ft (700 m) beneath the ground, some 3 mi (5 km) from the mine's entrance. How would they ever make it back to the surface?

Mine rescue teams face some of the most daunting conditions of all—there may be floods, explosions, or cave-ins at any time. The Chilean rescuers had to come up with their own scheme...

The 33 miners reached a small refuge chamber. Every other day, each person ate one biscuit and two small spoonfuls of tuna, and drank a little milk.

On Day 17, a drill from the surface reached a point near the trapped miners, and they were able to attach a note to it, telling the world that all 33 of them were alive and safe.

Shafts were drilled down and widened. With the help of U.S. space agency NASA, the Chilean navy built steel rescue capsules.

On October 12, a rescue worker was lowered into the refuge chamber. Up came the first miner, Florencio Ávalos. Within 24 hours, all 33 miners were safely at the surface—and the world rejoiced.

▼ The rescue capsule (called Phoenix 2) started to go down at 23:18 local time.

- 300 ft
- 600 ft
- Mine shaft
- 900 ft
- Phoenix 2 rescue capsule
- 1,200 ft
- Escape shaft
- 1,500 ft
- 1,800 ft
- Location of mine shaft collapse
- 2,100 ft
- Location of the refuge chamber where the miners waited to be rescued
- 2,400 ft

33

Looking GOOD

Humans have always put a lot of thought and effort into their appearance. Even when people wear similar clothes in cities around the world, there's still all sorts of variation, from wedding dresses, fashion statements, and performance gear, to military uniforms, traditional clothes, or religious dress.

Silver headdress
GUIZHOU PROVINCE, CHINA
Spectacular silver jewelry is worn on special occasions by the women of the Miao people.

Pearly king
LONDON, ENGLAND
Cockneys (people from the East End of London) used to decorate their clothes with pearl buttons. Today "pearly kings and queens" raise money for charity.

Masked reveler
SWABIA, GERMANY
In southern Germany and the Alps, the *Fastnacht* carnival is celebrated with weird masks and ribboned costumes.

Painted bride
KOSOVO/MACEDONIA
In the Shar mountain region, the brides of the Torbesh community have their faces painted for good luck.

Humans were making jewelry—in the form of necklaces crafted from strings of shells—more than 90,000 years ago.

Catwalk couture
PARIS, FRANCE
High fashion looks are paraded on the catwalk in stylish cities such as Paris, Milan, New York, and London.

Temple dancer
THAILAND
Beautiful costumes and headdresses are worn by Thailand's graceful dancers.

Stilt balancer
MALI
The funerals of the Dogon people feature masked and costumed dancers, some of them on tall stilts.

Feathered highlander
PAPUA NEW GUINEA
Fantastic feathers, costumes, and face paints are still worn at tribal gatherings in the mountains of Papua New Guinea.

Haka warrior
NEW ZEALAND
Hakas are traditional dances of the Maori people, still performed on ceremonial occasions. High-ranking Maoris used to have intricate facial tattoos.

35

The Art of PERFORMING

Shows and displays provide performers with an excuse to go that extra mile for the sake of their art. Many great creative types love working on a grand scale, or shocking the audience. And when it comes to pop music or the circus, spectacular and extraordinary sights are just what the public expects.

Making a splash
Between 2005 and 2007, Henry Purcell's opera *Dido and Aeneas* was staged by a Berlin-based dance company called Sasha Waltz & Guests. The 17 dancers performed the opening prologue underwater, in a tank filled with 9,000 gal (about 34,000 l) of water.

That's a wrap
Some of the most spectacular art installations of the last 50 years were made by the artists Christo and Jeanne-Claude. They wrapped up famous public buildings, bridges, and monuments. In 1971 they placed a 150,700 sq ft (14,000 sq m) orange curtain across a valley in the Rocky Mountains, and two years later built a 25-mi- (40-km-) long fence in California, U.S. In 1983 they surrounded 11 islands in the U.S. state of Florida with 6,499 sq ft (604 sq m) of pink plastic, employing 430 workers.

▲ *Dido and Aeneas*—the oldest known English opera still performed—was reinvented with innovative underwater choreography.

◀ In 1997–1998 Christo and Jeanne-Claude wrapped these trees in Switzerland in woven polyester fabric.

◀ Live Aid had the biggest ever global audience, all in a good cause. It was organized by rock stars Bob Geldof and Midge Ure.

The giant gig

In 1985, Live Aid rock concerts were held at multiple venues around the world to raise funds to relieve the famine in Ethiopia. Thanks to satellite television, Live Aid was viewed by about two billion people in 60 countries, and raised around $50 million (£30 million).

▶ The legendary skills of the Chinese State Circus.

Celebrated ceiling

The Sistine Chapel in Rome has a beautiful painted ceiling—the work of Italian artist Michelangelo. It covers 11,840 sq ft (1,100 sq m), with the nine central panels showing the stories of the Book of Genesis. The ceiling took around four years to complete (1508–1512), and over 4.3 million visitors a year continue to visit five centuries later.

▲ Michelangelo's masterpiece contains more than 300 figures.

Circus spectaculars

Animals are now rarely used in circuses. Instead, incredible human feats are being taken to new limits. Popular acts in both the traditional and the modern circus (which places greater emphasis on artistry, music, storytelling, and theater) include juggling, mind-boggling contortion of the human body, daring work on the trapeze and high wire, sword swallowing, and fire-eating.

Fun, Fun, FUN!

▲ The *Palio*—a giddy gallop in the center of Siena, Italy.

Fairs and festivals offer people a chance to relax and have fun. Traditionally, carnival permits outrageous behavior that would not be accepted at any other time of the year. There may be costumed parades, fireworks on a lavish scale, funfair rides, music, dancing, singing, and feasting.

Palio!

Twice a year the Piazza del Campo, in the Italian town of Siena, is taken over by crowds and colorful flags that represent each of the city's 17 wards. The event is a fast and furious, no-holds-barred, bareback horse race for three laps of the square. It is an exciting, dangerous contest, which recalls public games such as jousting and bullfights in medieval Italy. The race is known as the *Palio*, after the banner awarded to the winner.

Samba city

The world's most famous carnival parade and samba dancing extravaganza is in Rio de Janeiro, Brazil. The festivities in the city date back to 1723 and the highlight is the parade of floats that head for the "sambadrome." Each float is packed with members of rival samba "schools," flanked by dancers, all wearing the most fantastic, glittering costumes. There are costumed balls, parties on the streets and beaches, and everywhere fantastic drumming to a samba rhythm can be heard.

▶ Rio's samba schools practice all year round to prepare for the flamboyant spectacle of Carnival.